Gorilla Sales

ISBN: 1-4392-1245-7
ISBN-13: 9781439212455

Visit www.GorillaDung.com or www.booksurge.com
to order additional copies.

Gorilla Sales

How to Sell Anything at Any Time Regardless of the Apes in Charge!

Curt Redden

About the Author

CURT REDDEN stays on the cutting edge of sales and leadership training. He currently works with the senior management team of a leading global transportation service provider. Curt is currently based in China, and is responsible for sales and training for all firm operations there. Curt attained his Masters in Business Administration with an emphasis in International Business. Curt currently lives in Beijing, China, with his wife and twin children.

To learn more about his training and speaking engagements, please visit www.GorillaDung.com

Introduction

I want you to be successful in sales! This book is an effort to help you keep it simple, and immediately become more effective in selling anything, to anyone, in any market in the world, regardless of the challenges you might face. Whether you are new to sales, have been selling most of your career, or are simply looking for additional insight and tips to help drive further sales success, this story will help highlight skills that work!

In order to help illustrate points, we have chosen to tell a story that you might even recognize from your own company. While the characters and names have been changed, you may notice slight similarities with your own company or your own sales experience. I can assure you these are quite innocent, and are most likely purely coincidental.

In sales of any kind, there are best practices that just work, regardless of where you are, and who your target customer might be!

This book will focus on the things that work, and highlight some of the things that don't, in order for you to be more effective and pull through more sales! So before we begin, we ask that you keep an open mind and accept the story as you read it. While certain creative licenses have been taken, the following tale is one that is occurring right now in sales organizations around the world. I guarantee it!

Official Disclaimer

The characters presented in this story are not intended in any way to resemble actual people—or animals for that matter. Any similarities to actual people are unintended and assuredly coincidental. If at any given time you feel offended by what is contained in the story, please accept our most heartfelt apology. In addition, please take the added step of putting the book down so that you may seek immediate medical attention. This author can recommend several fantastic "colon hydrotherapy" treatments for both relaxation and cleansing benefits.

Based on a true story in a land far, far away...

∽

ROAD TO THE
WORLD OF CHIMPIONS

Road to the World of Chimpions

Many years ago there lived a colony of monkeys in what many considered to be a tropical paradise. There were pristine white sandy beaches and plenty to eat and life was generally good. Most of the monkeys worked at their largest employer in the jungle, Bananas R Us (BRU, Inc.). BRU had built a robust business around the region and were noted for their quality, delicious bananas.

A young monkey named Sam was eager to start his career with BRU's banana division upon graduation from the local university, Coconut Tech. Sam was generally unclear about what he wanted to do; he had majored in business, and desperately looked forward to pleasing his family with a rapid ascent through the BRU management ranks.

He had interned at BRU for several summers and was familiar with the product and the harvesting procedures.

Sam had always been good with the other monkeys, and everyone seemed to genuinely like him. As a young chimp, Sam had helped fund his need for buying video games, like his favorite "Donkey Kong," by offering beach-side massages for the older monkeys. He also had installed a complete "debugging" station. He had built a good business. When the BRU recruiter heard about Sam's early success as an entrepreneur, he told Sam that he should go into sales!

Sam didn't know much about sales, but was anxious to start a great career. I mean, he liked bananas, thought they tasted great, and he sure thought he could sell them. Sam arrived for his first day of work, and immediately started BRU's sales training program.

His instructor was an older baboon named Kantdoo. Kantdoo had held many positions at BRU and was due to retire next year. He had bought a little tree house in Malaysia, and was also planning to tour Africa in his new recreational vehicle upon retirement.

He spent much time telling everyone in new employee orientation about how BRU probably would not exist without his substantial contributions over the years.

He had once opened several key markets and inadvertently created the idea for banana pudding when he accidentally fell in an ocean container full of bananas several years earlier. His body was finally extracted from the ocean container using vines tied together. What was left was a banana syrup that many thought tasted great. Banana pudding was created, and the rest is history.

Over the next three weeks, Sam had to memorize much information on banana specifications and exciting new technology, which enabled barcodes to track inventory. He even attended classes on special testing they were doing with frogs from the land of Miagra to grow longer bananas. It seemed he was learning everything about bananas. Sam attended two days dedicated to safety training as well. It was titled, "Avoiding slips and falls and other hazards of a misplaced peel."

Sam also received a review and initial training on how to sell the bananas. It was an advanced program on selling skills that Sam was told was the best in the banana industry. It was called Monkeys Making Sales (MMS). He was given a really big book to read, and was told that he would someday get to attend a class on Monkeys Making Sales. But he needed to read the book first. Sam was instructed that BRU didn't like to spend money on training until they knew if new sales monkeys would stay at BRU. Sam read the MMS book every day so he could learn how to sell.

Sam was supposed to ask a lot of questions of his potential banana customers, uncovering potential needs for bananas, and then he could solve his customers' problem by selling them...bananas. There were a lot of different types of questions that would help him sell bananas. It all seemed pretty simple, so he was excited to get started.

Sam was eager and arrived at work before anyone else. It was Monday morning, and he was scheduled to be introduced to the sales team at the Monday morning sales meeting of the pond division. The first monkey he met was Alligator, or Ali for short. Sam thought Alligator was a strange name for a monkey, but Ali explained that she was almost eaten by an alligator on a sales call one day, and the nickname stuck with the group.

Ali had one of the better banana territories, and seemed very confident. She had worked at Bananas R Us for two years, and seemed to know everyone. Slowly all of the sales monkeys arrived with coffee in hand, and it was time for the meeting to get started. At exactly 9:00 a.m., the rope swing from another tree swooped in, and Sam recognized the area sales manager for the pond division from an earlier interview. He had a big head and long tail, and strode confidently into the room. His name was Toobifor.

Toobifor commanded respect and attention, and Alligator had shared with Sam that he had been very successful in sales. He had apparently been recruited from the circus after a successful stint selling peanuts. Toobifor began the meeting by introducing Sam to the team. Sam was nervous, but told the group a little about himself including his time spent selling massages on the beach. The group loved the "debugging" idea and asked if he could demonstrate. Toobifor interrupted stating that Sam was only to say his name and how long he had been with BRU. That's what is stated in the company manual, and that's the way they always did introductions.

The next three hours seemed like a blur to Sam. Toobifor showed a lot of PowerPoint slides (yes, PowerPoint Slides—this is a story) and a lot of numbers, but little seemed to make sense to Sam. Toobifor talked about improving hit rate (which Sam thought seemed violent) and controlling margins, but generally didn't seem to say anything about selling bananas.

The meeting ended with Toobifor forcefully saying that everyone needed to make sure they had enough sales calls and customer-related time for the day. Sam wasn't really sure what customer-related time was, but he was eager to find out. On the way out, Toobifor reminded them of the *World of Chimpions* contest. This was a big contest where the winning monkeys—the ones that sell the most bananas—go to Miagra Island, also known as Funtasy Island for an amazing vacation. Sam decided at that moment that he must win. He was a very competitive chimp!

Training for the World
of Chimpions Begins

Sam was paired up with Alligator for the day. On the way out of the office, Ali introduced Sam to Teddy. Teddy was the only turtle working in the sales group, although there was a big tortoise that worked in the banana pricing department. Teddy seemed very nice to Sam, if not a little shy.

Ali commented to Sam on the way out that Teddy had been around forever, and seemed to keep his head down. He had once told Ali the key to success was doing exactly what you are told to do all the time. If you look good on all the reports, they will not bother you. Ali had protested that she thought they were at BRU to sell a lot of bananas, and many of the reports Teddy referenced seemed to have little to do with sales.

Teddy had smiled broadly, and said that was the beauty of it. He continued, "As long as you get the reports in on time, and do all the things they want you to do, you can be a star at Bananas R Us!"

Ali had not understood, and neither did Sam.

Since Sam was new, part of his training plan consisted of other monkeys showing him the rope swings. They set off to visit their accounts. The first visit was with a rhino. He was upset that he had been billed incorrectly for last month's bananas, and that his delivery had been late. Ali spent the next hour calming him down, and he seemed OK after Ali offered some free bananas next week, and a token golden banana with BRU's logo on it.

The next visit was with a giraffe. He had recently started buying bananas from a competitor of BRU, and Ali wanted to know why. The giraffe unapologetically said that Big Bodacious Bananas (BBB) had offered better pricing. Ali tried to see if he would switch back to BRU if she could match BBB's pricing. He said he would think about it, so Ali agreed to send new pricing over by pigeon the next day. Ali told Sam she would have to fill out the pricing request that night for Nono, the pricing tortoise. Sam didn't really know what a pricing request was, but he was anxious to learn.

By then it was lunchtime, so Sam and Ali lounged on the beach talking about the morning, while Ali spent thirty minutes keying the customer visits into her laptop. (We acknowledge monkeys would not normally use laptops, but all of us thought the same thing about humans fifteen years ago.) Sam didn't understand why it took so long, but Ali explained that all the details had to be keyed in under a correct "marketing initiative" or Toobifor would be really mad. She entered the rhino visit under the "Yellow Forever" initiative, and the giraffe visit under "Longneck Attack."

Sam didn't understand, but Ali explained that all visits should have a marketing initiative and detail associated with the visit, whether it meant anything or not. Apparently a bunch of monkeys from the corporate office had thought that "Yellow Forever" and "Longneck Attack" sounded pretty cool. Sam recalled from that morning's meeting that their group was not making their business plan goals for banana sales, but the marketing initiatives seemed to be doing very well.

He knew he had a lot to learn about sales.

Ali also explained that they used a software system to record all their customer data. It was called "Customer Reports and other Unnecessary Documentation" or "CRUD" for short. She explained how crucial this was to BRU, and Sam better make sure he keyed everything he did into the system, or he would get into trouble. Apparently CRUD had been purchased by corporate BRU as the best solution for recording customer data.

Ali thought it was originally designed and intended as a tool to help the sales monkeys better manage their territories. "It is now nothing more than a really expensive time card for the sales monkeys," she said.

Sam didn't know what that meant, but decided not to ask so he wouldn't look stupid.

That afternoon, Sam and Ali had four more calls, and Sam noticed they didn't seem to be doing much selling of bananas. One call was a complaint that a delivery monkey from BRU had gotten mad and thrown monkey poop at one of the parrots mocking him. According to the incident report, the parrot kept squawking, "Polly thinks monkeys smell bad!"

On yet another call, they were told that unless they could lower their prices, all the flamingos would be switching to coconuts due to lower costs. The flamingos seemed a little arrogant to Sam. The entire time they were talking they kept sticking their necks out, and seemed to be looking down their beak at Ali.

What a frustrating day!

They also had to go see a lizard about past due bills because BRU's finance manager, Dodopay, had asked them to visit. Dodopay was typically anti-social towards the sales monkeys. All he ever seemed to care about was getting BRU's customers to pay their bills more quickly, or finding a way to deny payment of sales monkey expense accounts. The lizard Sam was visiting got very upset, stating that he had paid the bill, but he was still unable to get the past due billing issue resolved after two and a half years. He turned to leave, but Sam accidentally stepped on his tail, and it fell off and started flopping all over the room. The lizard became angry; he stomped out of the room in search of superglue.

Ali explained that BRU had outsourced their billing collection activity to a snake colony in India. While it was less expensive, all the sales monkeys actually spent much more time trying to correct bills and resolve customer concerns. It was also very difficult to catch the snakes, or talk to them without them hissing back.

While they were scheduled to make one more call to a prospective group of antelopes, Sam and Ali received a message via pigeon instructing them to return to the office immediately for an urgent sales meeting.

Toobifor entered the sales meeting and said, "We must sell more!" He was grunting loudly and was waving last week's sales numbers with his tail. Apparently, the global market for bananas was down, and results were not as hoped. Even though Ali's area had been growing at over 200 percent, her plan had called for 500 percent growth, due to a projected increase in Global Banana Daiquiri consumption that had been planned the year before. Ali commented to Sam that her banana business plan had been given to her by Toobifor. She had no input in changing the plan, even though she had already seen that strawberries were becoming more popular. She was aggravated because some of the numbers seemed very unrealistic, but Toobifor said the apes at corporate knew what they were doing. Toobifor explained that there were very complicated software programs that knew exactly what the sales plan should be for Ali. After Ali protested more, Toobifor finally said, we had no choice. They told us we'd have to make a lot more banana sales because of the "Gap." Ali didn't understand the "Gap."

Apparently the gap was the difference between what the apes at corporate thought sales monkeys should sell compared to any reasonable or informed plan of what an area can produce.

Toobifor concluded with a grunt of, "We just have to make the business plan!"

Unfortunately, as Ali had suggested, this year strawberries had become all the rage, and Strawberry smoothies and daiquiris were the new "in" drink for the animal kingdom. In addition, it was rumored that Moolafasa, Simba's great-great grandson, would be seen drinking a strawberry smoothie from Pride Rock, in Lion King 9, *Lions need Money too!*

Toobifor screamed, "None of these things are excuses!" All sales monkeys must make their sales plan for bananas. "No one's going to the "World of Chimpions" with results like these!

Toobifor was also concerned about inflation around the pond. A nice glass of prune juice now cost three bananas in exchange versus two bananas just a year ago. In addition, there were currency and trading issues between tribes, increased competition from Big Bodacious Bananas, and the cost of their production was up since the monkeys had unionized last year and fought for additional pension benefits.

Where's my Peanut?

BRU was able to successfully offer additional benefits to the production monkeys by placing the lower and middle management benefits under a coconut shell. This also included all the benefits for the sales monkeys in the pond division. In a lively display from human resource apes from corporate, they were able to show how the benefits were just moving around, but not going away.

In front of the assembled sales team from the pond division, the HR team pretended a peanut was their benefits, and then placed the peanut under one coconut shell out of three displayed on the table. They then moved all coconuts around really fast in a figure 8. Somehow the peanut disappeared.

The HR apes then explained that the peanut was still there, it just might not be in the same place. Ali thought about her benefits, and that just confused her more. She didn't think the peanut was there at all any more. In fact, she thought maybe the ape from corporate ate it.

In any event, Toobifor interrupted Ali's thoughts with a primal grunt of, "So how in the world is anyone here going to the World of Chimpions celebration if we can't sell more?"

His solution was that all sales monkeys needed to be busier and do even more! Toobifor stated: "As we may not be able to sell more, we have to look like we're really busy." He introduced a new program that he called the "Sales Monkeyment Initiative" While it would replace the time they normally used to work on top target banana accounts, he said, "We need to focus on something called execution."

Toobifor explained, "All monkey sales teams will begin daily reporting of all calls. They will need to know about all discounts needed off Banana pricing." Toobifor had been talking with Nono, the pricing tortoise, about sales monkey discount requests for their customers. Nono was not pleased with the quality of information provided about their customers, so he had added twenty-six pages to the discount request form. Nono had communicated that this would speed the process and ensure more accuracy in the data.

Ali leaned over and whispered to Sam that Nono had to approve any discount that they offered a customer. She continued that BRU was more expensive than most of their banana competitors, which meant pretty much all requests had to go to Nono for approval.

Unfortunately Nono was not the fastest tortoise around, and it normally took him at least a couple of weeks to reply with what discount, if any, could be offered to the customer. If Nono did not have the authority to grant the request, the request would be forwarded to the apes at corporate. Corporate approval normally took another couple of weeks.

Toobifor elaborated for the group that BRU corporate was concerned about how big the average banana sale was for the pond division. It seems they wanted to know a lot more as well. Toobifor stressed again, "These things are all very important! We need to report how much time sales monkeys are spending with their customers, how many new animals are they talking to in a day, and how well our existing animals are ordering more bananas. In addition, we need to know how much time all sales monkeys spend eating, napping, and pooping."

Next, he introduced something called funnel management for the whole team. Toobifor explained, "We can show how many bananas we will sell if we project with target accounts." He insisted that all sales monkeys place any opportunity, no matter how small, into the sales funnel. Whether or not the opportunity was real or valid, or even a real banana customer didn't really seem to matter to Toobifor. Apparently the corporate office wanted all the monkeys to do it this way.

Toobifor also stated that immediately all costs must be slashed including travel to out-of-the way customer locations, and certainly no gifts. Ali thought about the gold banana she had given the rhino this morning that he really liked.

Sam was now more confused than ever about how to be a great sales monkey. He wanted to please Toobifor, but honestly didn't know how making even more unsuccessful calls or recording a bunch of data into the CRUD system was going to help him increase sales.

All the things that he was told he should do seemed to taking up so much of his time. He was already using a couple of hours each day entering information into his computer so Toobifor would like him. He decided he needed time to think.

In swinging from tree to tree, he came across a squirrel named Fred preparing his evening nuts. After talking for a while, Fred could sense that Sam was upset. Sam confessed that he wanted to do well in sales at BRU. He just had to attend the World of Chimpions awards! But after all the training and the meetings he attended, he just didn't seem to know what to do. He wanted to be successful in sales, but didn't know how.

Fred responded, "I recommend you find someone who is already where you want to go. Who is the best of the best at selling bananas? Find them, and see what they do differently that makes them the best."

Sam now felt a little better, and decided to go in search of that monkey tomorrow.

"Find the Best and See What they do differently!"

Finding Abster

The next morning Sam asked Ali and the other monkeys, "Who is the absolute best in sales?"

They scratched their heads (also picked a few bugs off of each other), and all seemed genuinely perplexed. Finally, Ali stated, "I think it must have been Abster! Yes, yes, Abster was the best sales monkey we ever had, until he got promoted."

Teddy spoke up also about how good Abster was at sales. He exclaimed, "Abster could sell anything to any animal!"

He is now retired after serving successfully in banana brand management at BRU for a number of years.

Sam set off in search of Abster. He finally found the right tree after a long trek through the jungle.

Abster had a nice tree house overlooking the water, and was lazily napping on a hammock. Sam shook his tree knocker and called out Abster's name. He was prepared to do whatever it took to have Abster help him.

Abster awoke from his nap, and asked what Sam wanted with him.

Sam told him everything. He was new in sales at BRU, and Sam wanted to be the best. He wanted to go to the World of Chimpions, but he did not know how to get there. Sam wanted to learn from the best, and he was told that Abster was the best. Sam would do whatever it took to learn the secrets of sales, and asked Abster if he would help him.

Abster thought long and hard, and decided to help the young monkey. He told Sam that he would meet with him once per week in exchange for ten bananas each week.

The bananas would come in handy since Abster's pension had been reduced after the last downsizing at BRU. He vaguely remembered them explaining it to him using coconuts and a peanut.

Take the Ball

Abster told Sam that his first lesson would be about something he called prospecting.

Abster pondered and was amused that Sam did not seem to think he was selling. It seemed from Sam's perspective that most of his time was spent handling complaints about banana quality, billing issues, scheduling problems and handling customer requests and bananas that went bad. He was also distraught about all the time he spent reporting.

He told Sam that good sales monkeys find potential customers everywhere, at any time, regardless of what they are working on!

Abster started with the story of when he was a young monkey in school. As a young chimp, he had loved soccer. He and the other chimps would play for hours with each other, and sometimes with the giraffes and gazelles. They didn't like playing with them though, as they had too many feet to kick the ball. Abster's coach, a gorilla named Ruffulo, once grabbed him and said, "You will never get better until you learn the secret of the game."

Abster asked, "What is the secret of the game?"

Ruffulo then told him, "You must get to the ball first!"

Abster didn't understand, so Ruffulo continued even louder, "You must get to the ball ahead of your opponent. It is your ball, and if you aren't there first, you MUST DO whatever it takes to take the ball! It is your ball—now go get it!!! In the end, you will see who really wants it more."

Abster looked at an enthralled Sam, and asked what that meant to the young monkey.

Sam responded, "That you should take your own ball when you play soccer?"

Abster said he would help Sam with this one, and wrote in the sand with a stick.

Aggressively pursue your competitor's accounts. Be unique, be better, be faster, and want it more!

"It can be your ball!" Abster related this to all his customers that potentially needed bananas. He had to find them. He had to hunt for them. While there were many ways to do this, Abster insisted that he had to find it on his own.

Abster then told Sam to think about how he could work on taking the ball the next week at Bananas R Us.

Sam returned to work with new inspiration. He started looking for customers everywhere. When he finished a sales call, he would go see the other animals around, and even look for other herds that were grazing in nearby fields. Even if they initially told him no, he would persist and say if he could just have some of their time, he could show them how he could help them eat better, love longer, or save money.

The "love longer" idea was from Abster, and included a free sample for his customers of precious scented oil from the lands of Miagra, one of the nearby islands to the south.

Sam was excited as he was starting to get more appointments and was identifying more animals that were interested in talking about his bananas.

It was then that Sam was told he would have the opportunity to receive coaching from Kantdoo, who would accompany him on banana sales calls, and help him learn sales. Sam was so excited, and he was eager to learn. He just knew that Kantdoo would help show him how to get to the World of Chimpions.

Kantdoo arrived that morning looking at a picture of the recreational vehicle he was buying for his retirement. He showed Sam how it could fit twenty monkeys inside, and at least thirty riding on top. He was also pleased that the engine had been converted to run off of Rhino dung, so his fuel expenses would be much lower.

Kantdoo had a very long form with him, and none of it seemed to be about sales. The top of the form said DBR– Delivering Banana Results!

Kantdoo talked for a long time about how he had to do everything on the form to be good in sales. The form had so much information on it! It asked about all his scores on all assessments he had taken about banana products and selling.

Assessments were long tests that Sam had to take to show that he understood everything about bananas and how to sell them. The DBR form also asked about that funnel thing again, and how many banana sales he needed to make his business plan.

There were sections on his technology plan, strategy plan, retention plan, negotiation plan, and, of course, his revenue plan. There was a lot more on how much time he was spending with his customer, and did he manage that time properly. Sam asked Kantdoo what it meant to manage how much time he was spending with his customers. Kantdoo responded that Sam should be in front of his customers at least seven hours a day!

Sam really thought that was funny, because just filling out all these reports would mean less time with his customers.

They also talked about how Sam should key everything into the CRUD program. They talked about all of the things that Sam wasn't doing right and Sam seemed to get discouraged again. What was even worse for Sam, was when they went to visit customers, Kantdoo wouldn't say anything. Then after the call, he would talk about all the things that Sam did wrong. Sam kept asking, now that he had found some customers, "How do I sell to them?"

Kantdoo told Sam, ask more questions, so you can show them they need bananas.

Sam did not understand that at all. They know they need bananas because they buy from Big Bodacious Bananas, so it didn't seem to make sense.

Sam had to get back to the tree house early because he needed to talk to Nono. Sam was waiting for fifteen banana incentive approvals for his customers, and it had been over a week. Kantdoo told Sam that it was good to head back in early because he had a conference call with the apes at corporate on additional pages they were adding to the DBR form.

Sam found Nono, the pricing tortoise, down by the pond. It was sort of their break room. Nono was busy snacking on a flower. He looked up and saw Sam.

Nono was really mad. He showed Sam sixty-one places on the pricing forms that were not completely filled in as requested. He said it was not acceptable, and he would not get his discounts without complete forms. Nono slapped the whole stack of discounts requested on the ground in the mud and said, "No banana pricing for you!"

Sam could not believe it.

"But I need these returned, or Big Bodacious Bananas will win the business. I have already been waiting over a week."

Nono told him he would get them back when they were completed accurately.

Sam wanted to get to the ball first, but just couldn't seem to see it right now, and he wasn't sure Kantdoo or Nono saw it either, from what he had seen during the day. Even if he found more potential customers for bananas, how could he sell them?

The following week Sam had another meeting with Abster, and shared what he had learned from Kantdoo.

Abster replied that you can always learn something from everyone you work with. While you may not have had success, the key is in finding what you can learn.

Abster decided it was time for another story for Sam to help him think about how he can sell and make it to the World of Chimpions.

The Lion, the Parrot, and the Gazelle

Once upon a time a lion, a parrot, and a gazelle actually grew up together. They had become good friends in spite of their obvious positions in the food chain. One dry summer, food became more and more scarce. At one point, the lion finally looked at the gazelle with lust in his eyes, and said, "You know how sorry I am about this, but I think I want to eat you!"

The gazelle, who was fairly quick on his four feet, was deciding whether he should run as quickly as possible. After a moment of thinking, he decided there might be another way.

He thought about what the lion really needed versus what he said he wanted. He asked the lion, "Why would you want to eat a good friend of yours?"

The lion responded, "Because I am really hungry!"

The gazelle, trying to be very convincing, shared, "If you eat me, you will feel good for a few hours, but you will then be hungry again."

The gazelle then asked, "Do you think it would bother you after you have eaten your friend, and would you be lonely after eating me?"

"Why yes!" the lion responded. "That might make me lonelier, and I might feel bad after eating my friend."

The gazelle then asked, "If we can get you fed tonight, would you consider looking for another solution to satisfy your need for food moving forward?"

They were then able to use the parrot to fly ahead and scout for food. The parrot would come back to them squawking about where the food was so the lion could find it. In the end, they were all able to eat more.

Abster told Sam that he always had to focus on the needs of his customer. If he truly stayed focused on helping his customers get what they needed, and helped them be successful, sales would take care of themselves.

It is not always what your customers are saying they want, but rather what they truly need that matters!

Focus on
Customer Needs

Sam was back at work and thinking about the lion. It did make a lot of sense. Although he was fairly certain the lion would have eaten the antelope.

He also thought how that lesson applied to the monkeys he worked with at BRU.

What did Nono really need, and how could he help Nono so—hopefully—Nono could help him.

Sam made a note to ask Nono what areas were the most important for him to get the banana pricing back quickly and accurately.

That afternoon Sam had a customer call with an orangutan named Joe who was running a tiki bar resort down by the beach (OJ's). They met, and the orangutan, Joe, told Sam that he would use him for bananas if Sam could beat Big Bodacious Bananas' price.

Sam told Joe he knew he would have to be competitive on price, but he wanted to make sure he was taking care of all of Joe's needs, so they could have a great relationship moving forward. Joe seemed agreeable as he lounged in a bright red Speedo bathing suit. Orangutan Joe shared some things about his business.

Joe had been fine with the bananas from BBB, but he did share with Sam that sometimes he runs short when the hyenas come in from the plains to unwind. Joe shared that they loved "grasshopper shots" topped with banana shavings. Sam asked how often he runs low on bananas, and how it affected business.

Joe pondered the question, and reflected on all the great parties they seem to have when the hyenas were in town. While he personally disliked their propensity for games, like "hide the banana," they did seem to bring in some good business.

Joe thought about his business some more and realized that the hyenas dropped some pretty good items for trade, and maybe they would buy even more if he didn't run low on bananas. They were also a pretty rowdy group, and they seemed to liven up the place.

Sam then offered if he could commit to always providing an ample supply of bananas during those peak party times and have a competitive price, would OJ's use Bananas R US?

Joe thought about it, and agreed.

Sam had his first big sale! He felt great!

He relayed the good news to Abster, and shared what he had learned. Abster congratulated him, and reminded him that the exact questions aren't as important as just staying focused on what the customer needs to be successful.

The next day Sam was so excited that he planned to do exactly the same to continue down the road to the World of Chimpions! At his second sales call he was meeting with a seagull that had been given to him as a lead from one of the other monkeys. The seagull's name was Janice, and she was very unresponsive to all of Sam's questions. He was asking her about her problems, and all the implications of not buying bananas, but Janice just seemed uninterested.

After a while Janice said, "You seem like a nice monkey, but why would we buy bananas from you? We can go to the dump for little more than giving the guard dog an occasional scrap of bread. In fact, everyone has been happy, and we see no reason to change."

Sam relayed the entire exchange to Abster. Abster responded, "There is nothing wrong with the way you are selling. It is how you are selling, or the strategy in how you are trying to help your customer."

Sam was now completely confused. He thought he had learned something about selling, but how could he help someone that did not want to be helped?

Abster said that planning is one of the most important skills a sales monkey can learn. But even the word planning itself is overused. Realistic and actionable goals must be planned for every animal call.

Sam didn't know what actionable meant.

He continued, "Action means the customer must commit to something! How are you moving the sales process forward? What steps must you take to get to where you want to go?"

Sam interrupted, "But where do I want to go? I just want to sell some bananas!"

"The key is planning," replied a patient Abster. "On every sales call, the best sales monkeys think about what they are really doing at the customer visit."

What are they there to accomplish?
What will help the customer?
What will move the sales process forward?

What are you trying to do to help your customer, and advance the sales process?"

Sam asked, "So what should I be trying to do, and what is crucial?"

Abster responded, "What is crucial is talking about the ***right things at the right time, with the right animal.***"

In other words, if Janice was happy, were there other seagulls in her flock that might be tired of eating at the dump? Sam decided to try, and the next day went back to see Janice. Janice stubbornly introduced Sam to one of the elder members of the flock, Bill.

Bill had been around for a long time, and actually had been the one to locate their current dump. Bill was getting up in years, and the grey was showing through the hair around his beak.

After several questions, Sam learned that Bill had grown a little tired of always smelling like trash. He had been spending more time at some seagull mixers and had noticed that the lady birds were standing farther from him at the birdbaths. Sam seized on this to also ask if Bill was aware that bananas had been discovered to contain ingredients that helped with feather appearance and assisted with bad breath.

Bill was quite impressed, and committed to trying some of BRU's bananas starting next month. Sam had made another sale!

Sam also made a mental note to drop off some of that scented oil from Miagra as a token gift. He thought Bill might like it.

After relaying the news to Abster, he shared that he had learned something about "strategy." If you are talking to someone who is not interested, a good sales monkey has to find out who in the flock might be interested.

If you are going to the World of Chimpions, you cannot take no for an answer. Try everything you can and show persistence no matter how nasty the animal you're dealing with!

Banana Customers Must Live Up to Their Commitments, or Else!

It was the next week, and Sam was feeling good about his sales progress when he bumped into Reportalot at the office. Reportalot was BRU's marketing manager. When he first arrived at BRU, Sam had asked Ali what Reportalot and his team provided to help with sales and marketing for bananas. She really did not know what they did, but she commented that Sam would be getting a lot of monkey mails from him on information that marketing needed.

Sam was expecting that he would be congratulated by Reportalot for the OJ's account win. All the sales monkeys were asking about it. They said previous sales monkeys had been trying to get Orangutan Joe to buy from Bananas R Us for years.

Reportalot frowned and his big nostrils seemed to flare. It was obvious he was not planning to congratulate Sam. He did not even grunt hello. He immediately asked Sam about the update for OJ's contract compliance for last week. Sam thought about it, and remembered how he had to update BRU marketing every week with any customers who weren't buying as many bananas as they projected. Sam would enter this information into a different system from CRUD. It was called the "Customer/Contract for Bananas and Action Tasks or CBAT for short.

Sam quickly responded to Reportalot that he had both updated Nono in banana pricing, and entered all the information into CBAT explaining the situation. He had even responded to five monkey mails on the same issue. Sam elaborated once again that Orangutan Joe has a seasonal business. He buys a lot more bananas in the summer and spring when the hyenas are in the village.

Reportalot interrupted Sam, and said he would have to cancel his banana contract. "That account is making us look bad on the reports we send to corporate!"

Sam couldn't believe it. He told Reportalot that they would lose all the business back
to Bodacious Bananas if BRU canceled the
contract.

Reportalot's solution was that Sam should
cancel it and resubmit for a new contract
when the hyenas came back.

Sam protested that Orangutan Joe still
bought bananas even when the hyenas were
not in the village, and he would never get the
business back. Reportalot was not pleased,
and told Sam that he had better think of
something soon, because if not, it would be
canceled automatically. "I am telling Nono
that either this agreement is canceled, or it
should be restudied."

Restudied basically meant that Sam had
to fill out another twenty-seven pages of papaya sheets for appealed pricing and hope
that he received the same incentives back for
the customer.

Reportalot stormed off while scratching
his backside. He turned gruffly and also reminded Sam that he had to send in his CBAT
updates every week even if nothing changed
in his banana accounts.

Sam just didn't understand why the
reports seemed more important than how

many bananas they sold. He also didn't understand why he not only had to update the CBAT system every week, but he still received daily questions from Toobifor, Nono, and Reportalot on why some of his customers weren't ordering as many bananas.

While he was starting to feel bad again, he thought about what Abster had told him. Focus on customer needs, and be with the right animal, at the right time, with the right issue.

He decided right then that he needed to choose his monkeytude and be more positive if he was going to sell more bananas! He went back to work to fight for the Orangutan Joe account, and see how he could help more customers. He would update Abster with everything on their next visit on Friday.

Friday afternoon finally came, and Sam was eager to update Abster on all the things that had happened. He really wanted to hear what he should do next.

Instead of giving Sam answers, Abster told him a story.

The Baboon and the Longtail Boat

Abster was pleased with his young protégés progress. While Abster could sense Sam's frustration, he knew he was making progress. He thought it was time to tell his young friend about the Baboon and the longtail boat.

Years ago there was a monkey family that lived on a beautiful island and they had a large tree house. It was an island with an abundance of food, and there were plenty of great trees to climb. There were several fur optional beaches, which attracted a varied and entertaining group of animals.

Unfortunately, the waters around the island were rising, and the leader of their monkey tribe suggested they begin to search for a new home. The head monkey in charge knew of an old baboon called Ben that lived down by the shore. He knew Ben had an old long-tail boat that he thought they could buy.

A longtail boat looks like a canoe that has been stretched to three times its normal length. It is great for transport, and can operate in very shallow waters. It would be of much use to the monkeys. They could use it to scout for other areas and to leave the island when and if the water level ever got too high. He sent a young monkey named Mariah down to the area to try and find Ben and buy the longtail boat. Mariah was a cute little monkey, very talkative, and full of energy. Mariah set off one Saturday morning with several carts of bananas to buy the boat.

Mariah finally found Ben late in the afternoon, and expressed her interest in buying his old boat. Ben sized her up, and asked what in the world a little monkey like her would do with a boat. Mariah told him everything she knew. They discussed how the monkeys in charge thought the water might rise, and how they really needed a boat to ferry monkeys back and forth.

Ben the baboon had been trying to sell the boat for over a year. He started trying to sell after seeing a movie titled *Snakes on a Boat*. Ben knew it was just a movie, but he kept waking up in a cold sweat thinking about a boa wrapped around his neck. While he was desperate to sell the boat, he was also a good negotiator. He proceeded to tell Mariah what a classic boat this was in the area, and how it would be difficult for him to sell. He elaborated that part of the royal clan of ruling baboons had once used it to escape the horrible volcano eruptions years ago.

Mariah didn't know all that information, but asked how much he wanted for the boat. Ben looked very hesitant, and finally said," I really don't know if I can part with such a part of baboon history. But if I were able to let myself do it, how many bananas do you have there to trade?"

Mariah looked startled, and said, "Oh, all these bananas are not for the boat. I am also buying more food and a new Speedo for one of our sales monkeys to use as a customer gift. I mean, this is over a thousand bananas!"

Ben cut her off, and said, "OK, I guess I can let it go for eleven hundred bananas, but that is much lower than my last offer. I would also have to get a banana payment for each year thereafter to adequately compensate me. I am offering it to you because I like you."

Mariah said "I can't spend that much and I honestly don't know if it is worth it!"

Ben continued to reiterate that this was a classic boat that was part of royal baboon history.

After about thirty minutes, Mariah finally said, "Well, I guess it is a classic boat, and the other monkeys would be very impressed with the importance to the Royal Baboon family."

Mariah wrapped up the deal by agreeing to pay Ben eleven hundred bananas plus one hundred bananas per year for the next five years.

Ben the baboon had been employed by BRU as well, and was looking to supplement his retirement income. Ben still couldn't remember what happened to that coconut!

Abster finished the story and asked Sam what he learned about negotiating.

Sam thought about how Ben had asked, and found out as much as possible about Mariah's needs, while he disclosed very little. He told Abster that Ben had offered only those things that would build value to his case. He also continued with a constant theme, or that the longtail boat was a classic, and part of baboon history. He also seemed to have the power in the entire discussion.

Abster interrupted, "but did he?"

Ben really wanted and needed to sell the boat. Mariah should have been in control. Sam understood that Mariah had shared too much, and Ben had used that to his advantage. Therefore, he was able to direct or guide the discussions to his advantage.

Ben also had a plan, and, as most good negotiators understand, they must plan out in advance how many bananas they will take, and what is their climb away price, the price at which no deal is better than a bad deal!

Great Sales Monkeys are Great Negotiators!

Abster continued by saying that this example very much related to sales. "Whether you are dealing with your customers or the apes at corporate, everything is a negotiation. It is a combination of both competitive games, and how you can collaborate to make sure everyone gets what they need.

"It is just like your discussions with Nono and Reportalot. While you may not see it now, they really are trying to help you succeed. The key is in helping those around us be successful. The best sales monkeys understand what is needed by all animals involved, and focus on a plan to best achieve. He then finds a way to make it happen."

Sam now seemed to understand. Great sales monkeys not only learn to sell, and try to have a strategy for their top target banana accounts, they must also learn to negotiate very well. Sam decided he would read more to understand how to better offer solutions that were beneficial to both his customers and Bananas R Us.

* * *

It was now one month later, and Sam was feeling better. He was concentrating on having a positive monkeytude, and he was proud of his progress. He was working hard to be better. Although there wasn't much sales training at BRU due to cost reduction efforts, he read much on his own and continued to meet with Abster. He also tried to learn everything he could from the other monkeys around him that were having success.

He saw himself on the beach at the World of Chimpions being fanned by birds from around the world. He would have all the bananas he could eat, and would have a harem of help in picking bugs off his skin. He could see it now.

These were his thoughts as he arrived for the Monday morning sales meeting. Sam just knew he would be recognized for all his hard work and progress.

All the sales monkeys heard Toobifor at the next tree well before his entrance. He was yelling furiously that the juice shop Monkeybutts was out of banana java. "How could anyone focus without java?"

Upon Toobifor's entrance, all monkeys withdrew in anticipation of the dung that could possibly fly.

Toobifor started with last week's sales numbers. Their monkey team was under plan. He had just received the latest data and information from the apes at corporate via pigeon. More had to be done now!

What was worse, they were not having success in their "Yellow Forever" marketing initiative. Toobifor screamed that all potential accounts that were their largest banana opportunities needed to be noted with "Yellow Forever" immediately! Sam still did not really know what "Yellow Forever" was all about, but he made a note to cancel all his calls that day, and spend the rest of the day trying to change his coding in his laptop so Toobifor would be happy.

Toobifor also said that because they weren't selling enough bananas, corporate was providing new products and services that should be sold on every sales call effective immediately. Bananas R US would now be selling Band-Aids and bandages.

After extensive research from an outside consulting firm called Real Milking Company (RMC), BRU was told they were not approaching banana sales correctly. The global account manager from RMC, a cow named Bertha, explained that many animals apparently slipped and fell after eating bananas, so the Band-Aids would be an easy sell.

Toobifor stated that there were new programs from corporate to support these efforts. The new programs included simplified pricing from Nono, which that included only seven papaya sheets of documentation instead of twenty-eight, and a new commission package where the ultimate winner could possibly increase his or her banana pay by 1.2% for the year, if the monkey made a perfect score on the 15 elements needed. This all seemed very confusing to Sam, but he wanted to do well, so he would start selling Band-Aids on every call.

Sales Needs and Operations

Toobifor was also pleased to announce a new team had been created from corporate to help them achieve their goals. It was to be called the Sales Needs and Operations team. The SNOT team, as they would be branded in field sales, was tasked with analyzing all the things the monkeys did every day. SNOT would be everywhere and look at everything to help get the monkeys back on their banana sales plan.

The SNOT team consisted of a gorilla from the banana operations team, an owl from their banana engineering group, and a sale manager monkey who would be on special assignment from the big lake division. With incredible efficiency, it was not even two weeks before this team was producing eighteen separate reports to help Toobifor and the apes at corporate understand how they could increase sales.

Every report ranked and rated all sales monkeys on many, many different elements. All of these reports were said to be very important for the sales monkeys.

The key reports were a series of sheets showing sales Balanced Scorecard results. The BS sheets were used by Toobifor and all other sales managers to evaluate how well a sales monkey was performing overall.

Sam and Ali were amazed at all the things on the BS sheets. There were thirty-two separate elements for sales monkeys. Sam looked for a while and finally saw banana sales under one column. He asked Ali which ones were most important. There were so many things on the list for the sales monkeys. Teddy pulled Sam and Ali aside, and was giggling. He told them to look at who was ranked number 1, and they were shocked to see it was Teddy.

Sam exclaimed, "How did you do it, Teddy?"

Teddy had not had a big banana sale for several months, and was not making his banana sales plan. Teddy told Sam and Ali

that they had to focus on what they were being told to do by Toobifor and corporate.
This was how they could be successful. Teddy
proudly told them that he got all his reports
in on time, and he had great banana customer
contact time!

He also focused on submitting a lot of requests for banana pricing every week. Teddy
also made sure to sell whatever products they
were tracking, such as Band-Aids, and he was
diligent to have it all detailed in the CRUD
system.

Teddy also canceled all his banana con-
tracts if they were underperforming, so Nono
and Reportalot really liked him. He also added
a lot of new banana targets in his funnel
whether they were real opportunities or not.
Teddy was saying how he might actually make
it to the World of Chimpions.

Sam really didn't understand how to get
the World of Chimpions now!

Toobifor interrupted Teddy's comments
to Sam, by concluding that documenting everything and every opportunity in the CRUD
system was most important, and he expected
changes now. He also noted that due to BRU
results, and everyone's need to reduce cost,

all future training for product knowledge and all sales training would be canceled effective immediately.

"Now go make it happen!" he shouted.

Selling Band-Aids: More of anything is not always better!

After a couple of weeks, Sam was disappointed that not only was he not having success selling Band-Aids, but he was not having nearly as much success selling Bananas either. Work just didn't seem to be fun, and many of the other monkeys were upset as well.

Teddy was in the main office a lot, and rarely came out of his shell. They were spending so much time in meetings, and responding to questions from Toobifor and everyone else on why the sales monkeys weren't having more success. They were now having nightly meetings around the campfire with Toobifor to report on how they were doing with "Yellow Forever." Sam was starting to leave his sales area early to make it back in time for the meetings.

Amazingly, "Yellow Forever" was doing pretty well because all the monkeys had added many opportunities whether real or not to make it look good. This made Toobifor happier. While their actual selling results of bananas (and Band-Aids) were the worst they had been all year, "Yellow Forever" had actually been a success!

Based on those results and that program, they needed a plan that would work as well as "Yellow Forever." Corporate Bananas R US worked again with Real Milking Company and Bertha to develop something even more powerful to help all the sales monkeys. The Bananas R Us marketing manager, Reportalot, was excited to announce to all sales teams that they would be getting just the help they needed.

BRU was immediately launching seventeen new marketing campaigns and initiatives to help all the poor sales monkeys.

One of the thirty-three conference calls the next week concluded with an enthusiastic cheer from Reportalot. "We know at corporate that this is absolutely going to help you in the field! Just look what we did with 'Yellow Forever!'" He then spent the next four and a half hours explaining how the initiatives must be keyed into the CRUD program to ensure they were reported properly.

The campaigns included but were not limited to: Eating well—powered by your stomach, Banana Strategy Room, Banana Tracking initiative, Banana Band-Aid Power, Project Yellow Force, and a "re-launch" of Longneck Attack with 127 more PowerPoint slides to support.

While nothing seemed really new to Sam about any of these "initiatives," they all required additional reporting and meetings to discuss. Sam was finding less and less time to actually meet with customers. He was also confused because he was being forced to talk more about his sales calls per day, and his time in front of his customers as opposed to talking about where he needed help. He wanted to learn more about what was working, and what he should do differently.

It was very difficult for Sam. He felt so much pressure to make even more sales calls. He felt like he had less time to plan, and was even more rushed with his customers. In working with Ali, Sam finally started to figure out how to code the data into CRUD so the reports looked OK, but it was still frustrating.

Sam thought it was probably time to meet with Abster again, to seek his thoughts on how he could still make it to the World of Chimpions. Sam shared everything with Abster.

He talked about the endless meetings, the reporting, the BS sheets and all the time he was spending trying to justify what he was doing instead of BRU actually trying to help Sam increase sales or show him how to do it.

Sam had in fact had seven Banana Business Plan reviews in the last month. They always wanted to talk about why he wasn't doing well, and what he was going to do differently.

The banana division also had five different focus group meetings where the big apes from corporate came down to the pond to listen to the monkeys' sales group challenges. They really seemed to understand, and Toobifor helped by telling them everything they should say before the apes arrived.

Abster sat sipping coconut juice, and simply smiled.

Sam was confused, and asked, "Why are you smiling when things seemed so bad, and when I am so far away from the World of Chimpions?"

Abster responded, "What you are encountering is not unique in the world of sales. When times are down and demand for bananas slow, the tendency of the apes in charge is to manage their chimps even more. It is not unusual, and believe it or not, they really think and believe they are helping. They want you to be successful. It can be difficult from their view of reality, though, to concentrate on what will best help the team achieve their goals." Abster now seemed to be drifting back to another time and place as he thought about his own experiences.

He continued, only occasionally glancing at Sam, "Rather than commit to the training, and skills that are necessary to sell your way out of bad times, they look to manage activities even more, because that is simply easier. It is also what they know, and where they feel comfortable. It is also easier to quantify. We like to have numbers to look at."

Sam looked on contentedly and moved quickly to catch a dragonfly near Abster's tail. "They're very good eating!" Sam commented.

Abster continued, "Unfortunately, while the apes in charge mean well, they often cannot recognize that over driving reporting and increasing reporting systems can lead to exactly what they are most trying to prevent. They sometimes can't or don't want to see what is really happening to the sales monkeys in the field.

"Sales monkeys actually start spending even more time away from their customers due the number of activities they are having to document for the corporate office. As the big apes want their chimps to be even busier, they actually drive their sales monkeys to focus on smaller banana sales, as they produce quick results."

Sam didn't understand why a monkey would focus on smaller banana sales. Abster clarified that smaller sales are easier because you can do them quickly and show lots of activity for the apes at corporate. They are also easier in that they take less time. Customers can be set up rapidly, and may or may not ever buy anything."

Sam thought about Reportalot and why he was always grunting about the new customers that did not buy bananas. Sam wondered if this had anything to do with the problem.

"In banana sales, the pressure can be intense. But as the pressure on activities increases, focus will actually shift away from where we need it to be—in sales. These are areas such as the effort on trying to close good banana deals, and finding new and bigger opportunities that will pay off much bigger down the road."

Abster saw that his young friend did not understand all he was saying, so he shared with Sam, "You have to be different to be successful." It was then that Abster thought perhaps he could help Toobifor as well.

Abster wrote a note on a papaya leaf, and folded it over. He then told Sam, "Deliver this to Toobifor at your next meeting, and see if Toobifor will join you and me the next time we meet."

Reaching out to Toobifor

The note read:

> *Toobifor,*
> *I know things look bad right now, and I have been where you are. If you will come to me with an open monkey mind, I think I can help you.*
> *The Secret of Success in Sales is in all of us. It is not hard to learn, but it is incredibly easy to forget, especially in times like these...*
> *You cannot lead where you will not go, and you cannot correct what you do not see.*
> *Abster*

Sam delivered the note to Toobifor the next day. After Toobifor opened it, his curiosity was killing him. What did this old retired monkey possibly have to share with him?

He went with Sam to visit Abster at the end of the day, and all three of them sat together and drank coconut milk.

While Toobifor had a lot of questions, Abster interrupted his queries, and asked Toobifor, "Do you mind if I start with a short story?"

Peanuts in a Coconut

Years ago our monkey friends in Africa were being rounded up by the ugly two-legged things that walked upright. Abster continued that the two-legged things would take a coconut, and cut a little hole in one end, and empty out all the coconut juice, so it was now hollow. They would then put peanuts inside the coconut.

Since the hole was only big enough for a monkey's hand to fit though open, it would not come out with a fist full of peanuts. The bad two-legged things were able to attach a string to the other end of the coconut, and actually pull the monkey into a trap because the monkey was so preoccupied with trying to get the peanuts out. Believe it or not, the monkey would not release the peanuts, even though the monkey knew it wasn't working.

Abster then looked at Toobifor and asked him what the story meant to him.

Toobifor stated that whenever he was in Africa, he would buy his own peanuts.

Abster smiled, and stated that we all have to stay flexible in our approach, especially if what we are doing is not working.

He wrote in the sand.

Doing more of what is not working will not deliver different results!

The next week, Toobifor thought much about what Abster had shared, and he decided to change his approach.

Questions are Good, but the Right Questions are Better

At his next sales meeting, Toobifor decided to ask his team what they thought they needed to do differently so they could all get to the World of Chimpions.

At first it was apparent the sales monkeys were nervous. They weren't really accustomed to answering questions, except the ones in the banana business plan reviews.

A banana business plan review was where the monkeys from the corporate office and sometimes Toobifor would come to the pond division ask a lot of questions about everything in a monkey's area. Sam was told that they had always been conducted in the past for all sales groups, but they had them more often if they weren't achieving their monkey sales business plan. The business plan reviews were normally about all the different numbers, but they would ask lots of different things of the sales monkeys. Sam was originally told that these were to help him, but now he wasn't so sure.

Typical Banana Business Plan Review Questions:

Why are you crying?

Why did we hire you?

Why does your area smell?

Why do you flinch when I throw bananas at your face?

Why is that bad?

What are we having for lunch?

What is that bug on your bottom?

Why aren't you making your sales plan?

Why can't you sell more bananas?

What is your banana hit rate?

Why aren't you seeing more animals each day?

Where is the closest place I can play Monkey golf?

Where is my CowBerry?

Why don't you want to be successful?

what is for dinner?

Do you think you have enough in your banana funnel?

Why are your banana sales so small?

Banana business plan reviews could last anywhere from a few hours to a couple of days, depending on how lively and energetic the apes from corporate felt. The sales monkeys would normally spend at least a few days getting prepared for the review. The apes from corporate loved the PowerPoint slides and had a nice template to help the sales monkeys prepare. The template had thirty-eight slides, and lots of pretty graphs and charts.

Sam was confused though about why they had to fill in all the charts. It was all information he would have thought the monkeys at corporate already had. Plus, they never really seemed to be paying that much attention during most of the reviews and slides anyway. Most of the time they just seemed to be staring at their CowBerries.

While Sam did not have one, a CowBerry was a device that apparently the apes could use to see their monkey mail and use to talk to other animals. Sam thought they were somehow hypnotic, because even during their banana business plan reviews, the apes in charge would just keep staring at them. Everyone at BRU called the communication devices, COWS. BRU seemed to have acronyms for everything, and sometimes he had trouble remembering what they all meant. He was thinking about COWS and trying to figure it out…probably something like "Constant Overload and Worthless S…! He couldn't remember what the S was in the abbreviation. He would try and remember later.

Ali also was confused about COWs and how they helped the big apes at all. She commented after one meeting that she had spent five days preparing information for the sales plan review. She finally got to present to a room full of corporate apes staring at their CowBerries.

Teddy commented that Ali was not focusing on the positive effects. "Believe me, CowBerries help you get through your slides faster."

Sam and Ali just didn't understand Teddy sometimes.

However, everyone could tell that something was different about Toobifor this time. The team could tell that Toobifor was not asking questions like they heard in their business plan reviews. He really seemed like he wanted to understand.

Toobifor persisted with a lot of different questions for the team. After receiving little response, he finally asked what they needed to do differently to have more success.

Where did the team need help?

After what seemed like hours of silence, finally a few of the sales monkeys began to speak up.

Toobifor was at first a little surprised, and actually became shocked about what he heard.

Ali needed help regarding a few of her top banana target accounts, Sam needed additional peanuts for giveaway items, the new sales monkey, Eva, needed training on banana peel uses and selling. A few others were asking for credits that they could use to take elephant taxis to their more remote customers. Teddy the turtle talked a lot about the snakes in India.

Apparently they were suspending or shutting off some of their best accounts for billing errors. The amazing part was that Bananas R Us was causing most of these billing errors!

Even young Sam spoke up about all the time he was spending to key into his laptop all the things they wanted about his banana accounts! He was now spending over two and a half hours per day just keying data into the CRUD software system!

Several of the young monkeys had concerns about whether Nono and Reportalot cared about whether they ever won any new customers or not. Ali even spoke up that the only thing they seemed to care about was looking good on the reports.

Ali and Teddy both shared stories of getting many notes throughout the day from BRU marketing or the BRU accounting department requesting updates by the end of that day!

The frustrating thing to them was that often, this was the exact same information they were already spending hours keying into the CRUD or CBAT systems.

Nono the tortoise actually worked for Reportalot. They cited many cases that took weeks to get back banana pricing. They could not understand because the monkeys at Big Bodacious Bananas could offer discounts on the spot. They also talked about all the time they spent trying to justify to Reportalot why some of their customers weren't buying as many bananas.

It seemed that BRU did not trust them to do the right thing.

Ali also questioned the recent changes due to the cost reduction efforts. She had no budget to give customers gifts, and she wasn't even allowed to travel to visit potential target accounts.

She told the group about her largest opportunity in her territory. She had learned of a new circus that would be having extended performances at a village to the south. She just knew they would need lots of bananas.

But in order to get to the village, she would have to take a ferry down south, and probably stay overnight due to the distance and travel time. In order for Ali to complete the trip, BRU required that she complete a Travel Utilization and Request Documentation form in triplicate. This TURD form required approvals from Toobifor, Dodopay, and seventeen other apes from the regional and corporate offices at BRU.

The TURD form previously required approval at the manager level only, but additional layers of approval were recently added. The sales monkeys in the pond division were fairly certain this was changed with the goal of discouraging any animal from actually traveling for business.

Ali finally just gave up on trying to visit the new target account because she had yet to receive approval.

Ali looked up at Toobifor and shared, "I have sales of over one million bananas in my territory; you would think I could get authorization for travel expenses to see my existing customers and prospective customers. In fact, why do we even need authorization?"

They really wanted to help Toobifor, but they needed Toobifor to help them!

Toobifor decided he would try. He engaged in helping with the identified items the next day. One by one he worked on the areas where his sales monkeys said they needed help in order to sell more bananas.

Toobifor started doing everything he could to help facilitate more sales. He worked with other departments to try to streamline processes and remove barriers for his sales monkeys. He was trying very hard to help his team spend more time with their customers, and in sales-related items.

Slowly, over the next few weeks, sales results actually started to improve. They were selling more, just not fast enough. Toobifor still felt much pressure from the big apes at corporate. He thought it was maybe time to speak with Abster again.

This time Toobifor went alone. Abster was pleased to see him, and invited him in for some frog stew. Toobifor's big nostrils flared when he smelled the stew. He was hungry!

After dinner, Toobifor shared with Abster that he felt conflict because he was used to telling his people everything they needed to do. He felt like he was giving them too much freedom and that some of them may take advantage of the freedom if he was not hard on all.

Abster responded, "Many times throughout a monkey's life, less is more!" When it was obvious Toobifor was confused, Abster continued, "As in life, it is the same with sales success. Everything can't be most important!"

If there is too much Fruit in the Air, Some will Drop!

Abster suggested they play a game. The game was called fruit cocktail. The point of the game was to juggle pieces of fruit between them, slowly adding pieces until one was dropped. The first one to drop a piece of fruit was the loser. Abster brought out several baskets of oranges, coconuts, and apples. He told Toobifor that that they would start with just a few until he got the hang of it.

Toobifor was confident, and knew he could win. They started by tossing just a couple of oranges back and forth. Toobifor thought it was very easy to keep them in the air. Even as Abster added an apple, and then a coconut, Toobifor knew he could keep them in the air longer due to his focus and younger age.

He tried picking on Abster's age by making some derogatory comments about how things change as you get older. He openly discussed the challenges of digressing eyesight, loss of manual dexterity, loss of fur over the monkey's body, and even the inability to control flatulence in later years.

Abster was not thrown off his game though, and he continued to simply focus on the increasing number of pieces of fruit flying through the air. Beads of monkey sweat were now appearing on Toobifor's brow. Abster sensed his trepidation and asked how he felt.

Ever the confident monkey, Toobifor responded, "I could do this all day!"

But Abster could tell that was not the case. Toobifor was now becoming more tense. It was becoming increasingly difficult as they now had nine pieces of fruit flying between them. They were using their hands and feet and even their tails to snatch flying fruit out of midair and return it to one another.

This was the sign Abster had hoped for, and he signaled to the monkeys who had now gathered to watch. They had all gathered in the coconut trees above. As if on cue, they began to jump up and down in the trees, and suddenly seven or eight more coconuts tumbled down from above.

Toobifor could not catch them all, and lost focus on which ones he had been following.

All at once, he was hit in the face with an orange, and then a coconut. All the fruit then hit the ground.

Abster asked what he learned from their game.

Toobifor responded abrasively, "That was not fair, and there were too many coconuts coming at one time!"

Abster laughed and said, "This game applies to sales and to life. When too many things are coming at you, you have to decide which ones are the most important!

"Which pieces of fruit are most important? Because some items are definitely more important than others when prioritizing. As a sales manager, you have to help define and lead in that area for your sales monkeys. As a successful sales monkey, you must understand that for your own area."

But Toobifor did not understand. How did fruits scattered all over the ground have anything to do with how he could be better in sales?

Abster responded that the important concept is to focus on the activities or efforts that drive the best return on that effort.

Toobifor asked Abster, "What are those activities ? This seems like a game of riddles to me, and I want answers!"

Abster told Toobifor that the skills a sales leader required to be incredibly successful were not really different from his or her sales monkeys.

Leadership in Sales – How you can Best Support

1. <u>You should use your ears more than your mouth</u>
    As Toobifor did with his sales team, it is always better to ask than tell. Sales monkeys will also be much more successful any time they are able to ask their customers questions. These questions should lead to answers that help the sales monkeys understand their customers' needs. It also helps the sales monkey make certain he is addressing the real issues that are important to the customer..

2. <u>Focus and continually build sales planning skills</u>
As with sales monkeys, the need for effective planning is what the best of the best do differently. They know where they need to go to help their customers be successful, and continually refine their plans to get there.

3. <u>Always manage the individual and not the group, and always sell to the individual and not the group</u>
Every animal has a different situation. They have different needs, and have different things that are important to them. Both the best sales leaders and salespeople recognize that fact, and do not try to apply the same strategies to all animals. They also do not "sell" what is not needed, whether to their people or their customers.

4. <u>King Kong Principle: It's huge in sales!</u>
Always coach and focus on the areas that have the highest impact. The sale monkeys have to be committed to achieving success in the area. This

area is also known as the King Kong Principle.

Abster responded to Toobifor that he had to think about what really drove the results in his area. The King Kong Principle is the understanding that most of our results come from surprisingly small number of our activities. In sales, that means most of our sales come from a small number of our accounts. It means most of our opportunities can be targeted from a relatively small group of top targets. It also means that by focusing more in these areas, you can substantially improve your effectiveness and grow into a King Kong of sales.

Toobifor stared ahead, and said blankly, "Didn't King Kong get killed by the two-legged things flying in mechanical birds?"

Abster confirmed, but quickly stated that was not the point.

Abster told Toobifor that he would come to better understand what activities best drove results when he came to better understand his role as a great sales manager and leader. "The role of a great sales manager and sales monkey is to do whatever it takes to help your monkeys achieve sales success. What do they need most in order to achieve that success?

5. <u>Act as the trees in the rainforest</u>
Both the sales monkeys and sales leader have similar challenges. There are so many distractions to really staying focused on sales and growing market share. The best performers always try to minimize or eliminate distractions. They also look to maximize real selling time and time with their customers.

"Sometimes that means acting as a sales leader has to act as the trees in the rainforest." Toobifor just didn't seem to understand. Abster continued,

"During rainy season, like it is now, it can be raining very, very hard, yet we feel little water. The trees provide protection so all the animals can be free to work on their main needs. It could be gathering food or building shelter for our younger ones. If not for the trees and cover, many of the smaller animals could literally drown in the water."

Abster continued, "A manager's role must absolutely be aligned with the top banana goals. Helping sales monkeys keep it simple with focus on a few key goals, you will improve performance and ultimately what the apes at corporate are calling execution."

Abster challenged Toobifor to look at how he used his time each week, and each day to reach his goals. He challenged Toobifor on how he was helping his people as well. He then took out a stick and began to draw on the ground. Toobifor watched him write.

1. *Is what you or your sales monkeys are doing adding value or helping your customers in any way?*

Abster said that any report, activity, or request that does not directly help your customers or sales efforts should be eliminated where possible.

2. Does what you or your sales monkeys are doing each day help lower costs, or improve sales performance in any way?

If it does not, it should be eliminated. Trash it! Get rid of it!

Finally Abster talked about reporting requirements for the sales monkeys. Poor Sam had shared with Abster that he was currently completing nineteen reports weekly on areas ranging from his account visits to his progress in various initiatives and other goals. The amazing thing was that much of this information was already captured in the CRUD system, so Sam was really just providing reporting for data that could easily be queried. Abster told Toobifor that he should always ask the following question.

3. Does any monkey actually read or do anything with this information? How does this report actually help you reach your goals?

If that question cannot easily be answered, then the report should be eliminated. Just do it! Stop sending it out immediately, and recognize that at a minimum you have just saved your sales monkeys some time. Driving improved results in sales is about relentless focus on those activities that help us achieve our goals. An additional benefit to eliminating unnecessary reporting will also be improved sales monkey morale, as well as overall productivity.

Overall productivity and its measurement should be centered on the activities in the most important areas. But measurement loses impact when it is applied to everything. It is the same thought process when you use ranking and rating tools for any elements.

The more you add, the more you lessen your impact and focus.

The best sales monkeys are the ones who spend more of their time and effort in the areas that yield the highest results.

In other words, the best sales monkeys stay focused on the elephants, the lions, and the cheetahs!

The Right Mix

Elephants are their largest opportunities. Every monkey should have at least ten main elephants they are tracking. They know them well. They have to work on their elephants daily and weekly. How are they selling, and satisfying the needs of the elephants?

Lions are their largest and best customers. Every monkey should always stay close to their top five lions. Lions have to be treated with respect, and you have to ensure the lions are always taken care of in every way. They require nurturing, and you must meet and establish relationships with many of the other lions in the pride. If the pride is pleased with our monkey, they will continue to keep him around, and not eat him, or replace him with another animal.

Cheetahs are those customers most likely to run. Every monkey should always know their top five cheetahs. They are on edge and feel the need to go other places. Perhaps they are tired of our monkey, or disappointed in him for some reason. Staying close to the cheetah is crucial, because once he leaves, it is difficult if not impossible to ever catch up and get him back.

Toobifor stared blankly and said, "So keep my monkeys focused on their top ten elephants, top five lions, and top five cheetahs?"

"The right mix, 10-5-5!"

Abster said that focus on this ***10-5-5 approach*** would help the sales monkeys have much better focus, and help them know where they should be scheduling their time. It really is about better time and territory management for the monkeys.

Focus and Execution

oth Sam and Toobifor seemed like possessed monkeys. While some on the team thought they might have been bitten by something, or possibly had some outbreak of germs or disease, their energy was contagious! Both continued weekly meetings with Abster, and began to share what they were learning with the rest of the team.

Toobifor shifted from talking about all the activities the monkeys were doing, to actually being completely focused on their top target banana accounts. He had parties when new accounts were won. When Teddy the turtle finally won the Crock account, Toobifor presented him with a new shell. Emblazoned on the side of the shell were spray-painted teeth marks that said, "Bite here, if you love bananas."

Toobifor was listening to his monkeys, more than talking, and he tried to help each member of the team where he or she needed it, versus managing all monkeys the same. The team was hearing very little about the initiatives now, but they were hearing how the pond division was beginning to lead the company in new sales, and in keeping their older customers happy.

Corporate sales training from BRU had rolled out a new monkey sales training program to replace Delivering Banana Results. It was called Achieving Performance Excellence or (APES). It really simplified the coaching forms, and also the focus for the sales monkeys.

This training was about what the monkeys were doing to improve in their sales efforts, and stay focused on their customers. They were learning more than ever, and really beginning to benefit from the coaching and emphasis on sales monkey development and execution in sales.

Reportalot from marketing had been a tremendous help in the improvement in results. After the win on the orangutan account, he worked with Sam and Toobifor to figure out a way to structure the banana contract.

Marketing then refocused its efforts on providing more area-specific help.

Reportalot provided a simple program for the entertainment sector in the pond area, titled "Banana Bash—Party like a Hyena!" The program included new liqueurs, daiquiri mixes, and golden bananas for top customers! The sales monkeys were having tremendous success with help from marketing.

Reportalot had also worked with Nono to help speed up turnaround time on banana pricing. He helped Nono understand his role and goals as a part of increasing sales and growing market share, while still protecting banana margins. Nono then gave valuable feedback on how the sales monkeys can better communicate their strategy for winning new business so Nono could help. In return, the sales monkeys were gladly doing more to help Nono be successful.

In focusing on some other areas of success, Corporate BRU and marketing had also provided more resources to some groups where they had more banana sales. With input from the pond division, they provided assistance with something they called segmentation.

They had created a "FIRE" sales group that focused exclusively on frogs, iguanas, rats, and elephants. Through extensive research and help from Bertha at Real Milking Company, this was a great area of opportunity for current and future banana sales. They had learned from the monkeys in the pond division, that these groups had different needs, and were likely to want even more bananas in the future! It was already having some initial success. Most importantly, the efforts of all divisions of BRU were coordinated to help win this business and grow market share in this area.

Sam was excited about all the progress. He was talking with Ali and Teddy about how he was networking with all the animals in the kingdom, and had started getting even more referrals for BRU. He was planning better with his *10-5-5 customers*, and was really becoming known for his reputation of understanding his customers' needs. He was becoming a monkey advisor to them for more than just bananas and Band-aids. Sam read sales books nightly to continue to learn about how he could ask better questions, to both understand his customers' business, and to make sure he was helping them. It seemed all the departments at BRU were beginning to feel that growing the banana business was everyone's responsibility.

Kantdoo became an account champion. If he was working with a monkey, he had to actually be engaged with the strategy to win the account, and help win it versus just talk about it. Instead of spending all his time filling out Delivering Banana Results forms, he was using the new and improved APES methods to provide better focus on development. As these things changed, many of the younger chimps were actually learning a lot from him. Everyone had to sell, and did sell from top down. It was exciting!

Abster was pleased to see how Toobifor, Sam, and the team were growing. He was also pleased to see how the different departments were helping and working toward the same goal. As the different groups were becoming more aligned and focused on truly wanting to increase sales, and grow market share, they were making it happen. As they grew and learned what was working best, they would share with the other teams as well. Abster was so proud of their progress.

He shared with them at a lunch one day that they were both exceeding even his wildest expectations. It was finally time to talk about some of the monkey sales best practices that all sales monkeys should embrace. He elaborated that sales best practices were the areas that the best sales monkeys concentrate on in their prospecting, sales, and their strategy development for their customers.

Monkey Sales Best Practices

Abster again took out a stick and started to write in the dirt.

1. Planning is key

You have to make planning a priority for your area. You focus on your customer and what you need to advance the sale. Stay focused on your customer and not on Big Bodacious Bananas. While you have to stay in touch with what the competition is offering, it is much more important to address your customers' needs.

2. Network as much as you can

See as many animals and departments as you can with your customers. Learn about each of their needs, and how you can help them achieve their goals. Focus on your relationships with each group, and how you are able to help each one.

3. Use your team

At BRU, there are many departments and a support team to help you be successful. Wherever possible, you should be looking to ask for and get help to solve customer problems and needs. Your role is to focus on sales, so there are times you must have help with service issues, or other areas that don't contribute directly to growing your banana business.

4. Continually develop your relationships both outside of BRU and within

Stay positive! The best sales monkeys keep their commitments, and they do what they say they are going to do. This will not only assist with your reputation, but will help you ensure there are monkeys there to help you when you need the help. You must stay accountable to your lions, elephants, and cheetahs.

5. Win Business Faster

You can help accomplish this through better understanding of the customer and their goals and objectives. You can be a solution provider who links what they are trying to do with how bananas and BRU's other products can help with their goals. It is all about the business needs of your customer. Focus on that area, instead of the products and services at BRU.

Abster smiled, and concluded by telling them both that he expected even greater things from them moving forward.

If you both can take care of these things we have discussed, the rest of the items will fall into place. I can guarantee you will achieve your goals, and even make it to the World of Chimpions.

Fun is Good

As the end of the year was approaching, it became apparent that confidence and enthusiasm had overtaken fear and doubt in the pond sales group. They were working as a team and learning from each other. Sales performance and results continued to improve for the entire group. They shared what they were doing to win new business with each other, and they continued to help each other. The pond division was also losing fewer customers. It seemed that better focus on their lions, elephants, and cheetahs was actually improving their customers' satisfaction with BRU.

At one sales meeting, called exclusively to recognize some recent wins, Kantdoo, Toobifor, Dodopay, Nono, and Reportalot surprised everyone by leading the team in a new dance called the Monkeyrana. Toobifor was starting to learn that sales can be fun if you let it!

"Less is more, HAVE FUN!"

Sam Heads Toward the World of Chimpions

After the Monkeyrana, Toobifor called everyone together for an important announcement.

He talked about how proud he was of the group for their progress and effort. He detailed most monkeys' accomplishments on the team in either beating their banana sales plan, or in the progress that they had made toward their goal.

Finally he said, "But one monkey among us has qualified for the greatest of all prizes!"

Toobifor announced that Sam would be heading to the World of Chimpions! He also praised the monkeys in the group that had done well, but did not quite qualify. He knew that Sam would represent the group well, and next year, they would all plan to join him.

Sam could not believe he had done it. On his way back to his tree that night, he thought about all the monkeys who had helped him.

He felt like he had paid attention. He had tried to work on his elephants every day. He managed his lions very carefully. He did not let his cheetahs run away. He had learned to be the first to the ball, and if he was not, he would do everything in his power to take it away. Once he was with his elephants, he stayed focused on what they most cared about.

He knew by making those around him successful, he would be successful. Whether selling bananas or Band-Aids, he made sure that BRU was absolutely satisfying the animal needs, or at least positioned them so that it appeared that way. He did not talk about BRU's products that did not matter or help his customer. He also tried to share what was working with the other Monkeys on the team.

He also realized how much he had come to respect that Toobifor was also now part of the team. While there were still times that they had to get papaya leaf reports in quickly, it was not as often, and there were some pieces of fruit that hit the ground.

They were working better as a team, and Toobifor seemed to care about them.

Everyone seemed to understand the goals, and it was all related to their top banana targets (elephants), their largest accounts (lions), and those most at risk (cheetahs).

Everyone seemed to be having more fun, and working together to achieve the goals.

Back at his tree, Sam dreamed of the trip to come.

Sam arrived on Miagra/Funtasy Island in January, and his pelican lift was greeted by a little hermit crab named Craboo. The World of Chimpions was more than he could ever have hoped to achieve in his first year. Toobifor was there, as well as very proud apes from Bananas R US corporate. Everyone seemed to be beaming with pride and seemed so happy with what all the sales monkeys present had accomplished.

Their keynote speaker at the Gala World of Chimpions dinner was announced as follows by the monkey of ceremonies:

"It is our pleasure to introduce the best selling monkey that Bananas R US has ever seen. The only monkey in history to have attended every World of Chimpions award banquet since first introduced." The monkey of ceremonies clarified, "Although the World of Chimpions was canceled every other year due to cost containment initiatives, he would have still qualified in every year. In any event, he is the only monkey ever to have attained the prestigious "Golden Banana" which paid homage to his perpetual excellence in Sales." The Monkey of Ceremonies then yelled out, "Please give it up for Abster, the one, the only, the true Sales Gorilla!"

It was then that Abster swung up to the podium. The room erupted in thunderous clapping and "hoots" of "You the monkey!!!" Apes and monkeys gone wild! It was a great scene.

Abster started by calming down the crowd. He began with the following:

"While you are cheering for me, it is really these top-performing Monkeys that deserve our applause. They are not only the best of the best, but they have shown they can move bananas in a bad economy. I know that even better days are ahead."

He explained how his success and those he had seen do well have common traits. Those were the sales monkeys who stayed focused on helping those around them be successful. Those monkeys would always be able to sell enough Bananas!

"If you were unable to sell successfully to one animal, you continue to explore who in the organization might have needed your help, and eventually our products. But above all else, you maintain the Monkeytude, that you can do anything.

"Understand you are always negotiating, and stay positive to make our organization do things they may not want to do, and also to help their customers. That positive effort, regardless of what occurs, like an alligator snapping your tail, will always bring you sales success. Finally, have fun in all that you do.

"Now someone crank the crickets, it's time to do the Monkeyrana!"

Sales Gorilla in the Making

The next day for Sam was a glorious sun-splashed day. Late in the afternoon as the sun was setting over the south sea of Funtasy Island a tired Sam reflected on how he arrived.

Sam lay in a hammock thinking of what he had learned so far, and how he would always be different. He thought about what Abster had said. By helping those around him be successful, including his customers, he now understood that those efforts would mean success for him. Everyone is always selling something, and Sam thought about how much fun it would be for him as he continued to get better.

He fell asleep in the hammock that night realizing that if a monkey like him could become better in sales, then surely all the animals in the kingdom were worthy of the World of Chimpions if they only tried! Regardless of what happened, he knew he would always stay positive, and always help his customers.

He knew that one day he could grow into a great sales gorilla!

All the monkeys (and other animals) live happily ever after.

The End of this Story

* * *

(Now Reflections after World of Chimpions)

Back from the World of Chimpions

This story was a lighthearted view of what the best salespeople and managers do differently. Let's review a few of the key areas, and provide a little more explanation in areas that might not have been readily apparent in the story.

Achieving success in sales is about relentless focus on customers and their needs.

Whatever your product or service, it is not about your products or services or the features of those products. It does not matter to your customer.

The best salespeople recognize that if they can genuinely help their customers solve a problem, make their life easier, or bring value above how they are currently doing business; the salesperson dramatically increases their ability to close a sale.

They utilize well-planned questions that help explore their customers' true needs, and look for the best ways to satisfy those needs. They are competitive and understand they must differentiate themselves from other salespeople and companies. How can you be creative and memorable to your customers? The best of the best focus on key areas for skill improvement and focus for growth. Some of the areas with highest impact were highlighted in the story, and are found in the following pages.

Prospecting

The best sales people get to the ball first. If it is not their ball, they take it. OK, what does this really mean? Prospecting is all about networking and increasing your pool of qualified accounts. Who could need your service, and who could find value in your offering? Use everything and everyone to make prospecting part of your daily life and a build a strong foundation and make it a habit! If you have great success with an account, ask for referrals! If you have no leads, follow your competitor. The best salespeople understand they will hear 'no', but recognize they need many rejections before they get to the 'yes'. They are or learn to get comfortable with cold calling both in person, and on the phone. They embrace prospecting as part of the job, knowing that it will pay huge dividends down the road.

They learn how to be brief and memorable. They are prepared and have researched their prospects before calls. They have basic understanding of how their product can help, and always define their solutions in terms of benefits to the customer. Even their generic prospecting messages whether on the phone, or in person are structured to make their prospect want to hear more. They always look to advance the sales process, without making prospects feel like they are being sold.

Sources are everywhere for the good salesperson. They use present customers, internal leads from within their company, the Internet, Yellow Pages, their competitors, networking groups, and trade shows/specialized magazines to name a few. The difference is they act. They follow up on leads daily to ensure they are growing their base and fighting to take the ball if they do not have it!

They also know that objections will be part of the process. They are ready with responses to the most common objections, and fight to overcome. If they do not, they still have fun trying!

Selling Skills

There are as many different sales training methodologies available as there are "Kantdoos" in the real world that have never sold anything. Somehow these groups, both internal and external to your organization, will profess to teach you everything you need to know about selling. The common elements of the best programs are the focus on the needs of the customer and asking versus telling.

Effective selling skill is really about listening more intently, and understanding both your customers' personal and professional needs. The best salespeople actually talk much less than their customers. They do this though better planning and questioning skills.

It really is about the power of effective questioning that explores your customers' challenges and that ultimately allows the salesperson to present a solution or product as a fantastic benefit to the customer. They effectively help build the problems of the customer to a point where the cost of the solution is much less than not addressing the problem.

They also stay focused on "advances" on each call, or making certain they continue to move the sales process forward. We could even consider these many "mini-closes" where the customer makes specific commitments along the sales process that moves them toward eventual commitment. With better understanding and usage of selling skills, these people drive shorter sales cycles, and ultimately better hit rates.

The best salespeople almost always find a way to define customer problems in areas that their product or service can also help. These could be areas such as improving/increasing sales, improving/increasing customer service, or decreasing overall costs. They also do not reinvent the wheel. As Sam did with Abster, they seek mentors who have already achieved the success they desire.

Product knowledge is important, but ultimately less important than staying on your customers' agenda, and helping them achieve their goals.

Strategy Skills

On his way to the World of Chimpions, Sam learns about the importance of addressing the right issue with the right person at the right time. While effective strategy is about much more than that issue alone, it is a fantastic place to start. In larger and more complex sales, salespeople recognize that there are many other risks involved in large purchasing decisions. They understand they need a well-planned and orchestrated approach to improve their likelihood of success.

They consider the changes in the customer's business and process, both currently and over time. It is about using effective selling skills, to help their customers better recognize the needs, and then help frame their buying criteria. As many more people may be involved, the great sales gorilla ferociously differentiates himself from the competition.

He learns what strengths the competition brings to the customer and more importantly how the customer views those strengths in relation to his own offering. He normally does this emphasizing his organization's key strengths that most closely align with the client's needs. He demonstrates capability, by offering third-party references, demonstrations, and unfettered confidence and commitment to the value of his product.

Price concerns are handled directly, and with strategy. The best salespeople understand that early in the sales cycle they must acknowledge and defer price concerns. They communicate clearly that they know they must ultimately present a competitive offering.

However, before they reach that point, they must understand what the true needs and/or the scope of the solution will be that will best serve the customer. If price concerns continue to surface later in the sales cycle, they will explore the issue. They seek to understand and learn whether these price concerns are legitimate or driven by other factors. These could include legitimate negotiation issues, or possibly the fear of change, or the risk involved. He will then respond appropriately to resolve concerns.

He understands he must be competitive in price, but defines solutions in terms of the value that it brings for the customer, and never apologizes for being more expensive if that is the case. A great salesperson effectively quantifies benefits wherever possible for maximum impact. The best salespeople show the savings and impact in real dollar terms that the customer can understand. You get what you pay for!

He helps the customer make a decision, and absolutely asks for the business. He typically proposes conditionally, with several people or departments, to ensure he can bring them all to the same place at the same time.

Strategically, he manages accounts even better once he has won the business.

They are his lions, and he treats them like royalty, and ensures they will recommend him highly to other elephants. As with most businesses, many things can change over time, and new opportunities or threats are always near. The best understand that threat, and remain vigilant in improving their relationships with their top accounts.

They extend the depth and breadth of their contact into other departments, and other contacts throughout their clients business.

Negotiation Skills

While this story is certainly not an overview of effective negotiation strategy, it is important to highlight this area due to the importance to all salespeople. We are always negotiating. Whether you are negotiating externally with your customers, or internally with your own organization, those who ask for more get more. A well-planned negotiation strategy is essential for the best results in all sales.

This strategy should recognize the difference of when your negotiation is competitive in nature versus more relationship oriented. A competitive example might be defined as the classic win-lose situation. Examples of competitive negotiations would include buying a used car, or any purchase that is characterized as a one-time no-future-relationship moving-forward scenario. The more likely example for salespeople is when there is an ongoing relationship. This should be a more relationship-oriented negotiation. Both types require different sets of behaviors to achieve the most success.

The best negotiators tend to believe in their products or solutions and show that belief with passion. As Ben did with Mariah in the story, they manage information well, and they always reach for the sky, or set high, but reasonable targets. They understand the positioning of real power at the table, and explore and understand all the areas where they could seize more power. It could be because of the needs of the customer, or perhaps the situation. It could be because of changes over time at their customer's location. What has changed in the business environment? Are there new key players in your customer's organization? Are there new threats or opportunities that your customer needs to address? How can you help them achieve their goals and still get what you need from the negotiation process?

Above all else they stay close to what the customer needs versus what they say they want. There are many ways to satisfy a need, but only one way to satisfy a want.

It would be highly recommended to continue to learn as much as you can, both from the best negotiators in your field and outside study. It will serve you well over your career in sales and life.

Many people feel there is only one perspective that matters and that is the customer.

While that is true, effective negotiation is really about improving your understanding of what is really needed by both parties, and working toward satisfying those needs.

Final Thoughts and Gorilla Sales Action Steps

We have reviewed much about what the absolute best sales people do differently. One concept introduced in the story was the King Kong concept. Often in sales, this concept might be known as the Pareto Principle, or the 80/20 concept.

As a review, this is basically the belief that 20 percent of your efforts yield 80 percent of your results. Translated for sales purposes, that means 80 percent of your current revenue, comes from 20 percent of your accounts. (lions) Eighty percent of your potential new business comes from 20 percent of your targets. (elephants) It also means in general that 80 percent of your productivity in sales comes from 20 percent of activities that you complete daily and weekly.

This book has highlighted those activities which have been proven to be the ones that yield the highest results in sales. While you must always juggle many pieces of fruit, the key is in deciding which ones you can drop occasionally and still be successful. While you may have your own list of the items you can drop, they can include items from many different areas.

The key point is to let them drop. The message here is that the top performers in sales understand that from a time management perspective, not all activities are equal. They reduce or eliminate where possible all those things that do not help them get to where they want to go!

Activities the best sales people attempt to limit could include any of the following; internal requests, conference calls, internal meetings, and possibly knee-jerk management changes in direction and/or marketing initiatives. These are just a few. Literally hundreds of other area distractions from achieving sales success can appear in your daily work.

Perhaps distractions come from quick or tactical changes requested in what you focus on because your organization is not providing clear leadership and direction. It could be countless (and needless) internal requests for information. This type of over reporting is often ingrained in the organization. Unfortunately, while some basic reports often arise simply to satisfy simple queries, they are hard to destroy or make go away once implemented. As a sales manager and top performing salesperson, you should challenge the necessity, and whether it adds value to sales performance.

Any reports and action of this type should somehow have value for the customer. Does it improve quality or service? Does it make you more responsive to your customer? Does it speed up decision making, or encourage innovation and higher performance? Is what you are doing somehow leading to decreased costs, or improvement in your key goals? If it does not, discard it or file it. These are preferably filed in the circular one under your desk.

If in the end, action is still required as mandated by your organization, or your boss begs you to complete, just do it! If you can delegate it, please do. But commit as little time, effort, energy, and brain power as possible to get these items dispatched. Just do it, delegate it, or discard it immediately!

The key for you as a top performer is to stay focused on the areas that will yield top sales results. Don't worry about the other stuff! Don't let it bother you, and absolutely do not let it waste your time. It will not change!

Nothing should be allowed to alter your focus and commitment to these sales best practices!

By focusing on your customers and your skills as a salesperson, you will differentiate yourself in the field, and will attain much higher results in sales and retention with your customers. The people who are leading sales organizations truly want that result. It is up to you to maintain focus and positive attitude regardless of other factors.

Whether you are in sales as a career or not, we are all selling something. In order to be a true sales gorilla there are things you can do differently to maintain absolute focus on the goal.

Success in sales really should be simple and fun. Somehow people and organizations all over the world keep finding ways to make it more complicated than it needs to be.

While we have detailed some of the critical items, it is important to wrap up with some of the things that are most important. These are some of the pieces of fruit that we can never drop. We will call these our Gorilla Sales Action Steps. Some would view these as the sure ways to ensure you make it to your own World of Chimpions!

Gorilla Sales Action Steps

1.   Make those around you successful
While true in many areas of life, it is cru-
cially important in sales. This includes
your coworkers. They might need your
help understanding these truths, and
your customers who need to benefit from
your product. I would add your family as well. The more successful you can
make your team, the more successful you
will be!

2.   Make your boss successful
We have all worked for a Toobifor at
some time, or perhaps you are working
for him or her now. Always understand
the needs of your leader. You can satisfy
his or her needs and also stay focused on

those things the best salespeople do differently.

3.   Get and/or keep an absolutely positive attitude regardless of any external or internal events

Everyone around you feels it, and there is a direct correlation with the positive nature of your attitude, and your ultimate attitude in sale success.

4.   Your lions and elephants are your livelihood

Fight for them with your life. We cannot overemphasize the need to stay close. **Think 10-5-5!!!**

5.   Price will always be important on some level

Your relationship with your elephants, lions, and cheetahs will always be more important! People will always do business with people they like! The best salespeople always find the most effective way to position value over price. They quantify that value wherever possible for maximum impact.

6. Invest in the prospecting and networking skills that will be the seeds of tomorrow's growth

If you are not yet comfortable with prospecting, please seek to both improve your skills, and force yourself to practice daily.

7. Be a solutions-oriented salesperson
Both with your customers, and internally in your organization, look for the ways to get things done versus complaining about what you cannot change. Customers need solutions that help them accomplish their goals. It could be a new approach, or something different in many people's eyes. However, it is up to you to sell it both internally and externally. Never forget that it is up to you and not your company! You are accountable for your own success or failure.

8. Persistence and more persistence!
Think of how young children fight for what they want. If you have recently told a five-year-old forty-nine times that he/she can not have the ice cream cone, think how that could apply to your sales efforts.

9. Continuous learning

Be dedicated to continuous learning to become better in sales. Read everything you can get your hands on, with particular emphasis on improving prospecting, selling, and negotiation skills. Watch and learn from those that are already the best.

10. Embrace monkey sales best practices, and sales leader best practices

As detailed in the story, they really do work! While many salespeople, including myself over the years, despise planning, it can make a huge difference in your ultimate success. Planning for your top calls, and how you will advance the sale will make you more productive in all your efforts. The improved use of networking, and the utilization of whatever team you have available. This will give you more time to focus on what you need to do which is...selling. The best salespeople know that relationships matter, and continually develop them inside and outside their organization.

Finally, they win business faster! They accelerate opportunities by staying focused on their largest elephants and their needs. They maintain focus on the value to the customer defined in those needs rather than the price of their product or service.

If you are a sales leader, it is essential to adapt your management style to each member of your team. They all have different personal and professional needs, and will perform better if you manage accordingly. While we often say it is better to ask than tell, it can be difficult to implement. Your team can help you get to where you need to go, but you need to be listening for the answers to be revealed.

OK, acting as the trees in a rainforest is a little corny, but the message is powerful.

Keep or reduce distractions from the field where possible. The role of a successful sales leader is to spend as much time as possible coaching and leading the team. It is coaching and leadership in these areas that most deliver business impact and sales results.

One more bonus sales leader and sales-person best practice. (Just so you can get your money's worth—this tip alone is priceless!!!)

Trash your CowBerry if at all possible. Do you really need to be that connected??? As a salesperson, try to refrain from ever using a CowBerry in front of customers or on a call. It gives the impression that, oh, I don't know—maybe that you are completely uninterested in anything your customer might say.

If you are a sales leader, the same thought just might apply to you as well. One more thing—if you ever find yourself presiding over a banana business plan review and you get that uncontrolled urge to grab your CowBerry to get caught up on your e-mail, why not try this therapy below instead.

Take out a Post-it note, and write:

I am bored and am not interested in anything you have to say, nor do I care about you or your challenges. I am here because I am checking the "area business plan review box or whatever unnecessary meeting this might be."

I care much more about me and my career than I will ever care about all you lowly sales monkeys.

Promptly stick the Post-it note on your forehead, and wear it through the rest of the meeting.

It will have the same effect as working your e-mail for the rest of the time anyway, and communicate the message much quicker to your team.

Focus in just a few of these key areas will absolutely deliver in increased selling time, improved sales force morale, and ultimately performance of your sales results.

11.   In closing, one final thought. Have fun in all that you do!

If you cannot do this, at least learn to fake it. Positive energy will flow, and it will help you more than you can possibly realize!

Best of luck in growing your sales and helping your customers be successful!

A World of Chimpions awaits you!

Acknowledgements

I recognize that these thoughts of appreciation may have little importance to you, unless you are either related to me, or you're still in the bathroom and have run out of reading material.

First, I would like to thank the many partners I have worked with at UPS over the years. It is a fantastic organization that has been blessed with many talented current and former employees. This story is not necessarily about UPS, or any specific company for that matter. It could easily be about any organization engaged in sales on any level.

Several groups, including the American Society for Training and Development, were instrumental in lending both insight and expertise. While there may be times that the story appears to be making fun of certain departments or issues, it was not intended to be malicious in any way. It is not my intention to minimize any business contributions from any department in any area.

This story was really about having fun, and providing a different perspective on sales best practices in a different way. This book has been about what the best salespeople do differently to deliver superior results, and nothing more.

To my parents, I want to thank you, and let you know that the counseling bills have finally been paid off. To my wife's best friend, Judi, I want to thank you for helping me believe that most attorneys really are decent people. To the family dog, Ody, I want to thank you for eating my favorite Crocks, instead of the flash drive containing this book.

Finally, I would like to thank my children, Sam and Aly, and my wife, Abbey. They are very special people who also manage to put up with me. If life is a roller coaster, there is no group I would rather be taking along for the ride!

No one ever succeeds alone. There are many others to thank including you as you read this book. I thank you and wish you the very best.

Made in the USA
Lexington, KY
16 December 2009